BEAUTY'S TATTOO

BEAUTY'S TATTOO

Cathy Colman

TEBOT BACH • HUNTINGTON BEACH • CALIFORNIA • 2009

Cover image: supplied by Inmagine
Design, layout: Melanie Matheson, Rolling Rhino Communications

ISBN 13:   978-1-893670-41-9
ISBN 10:   1-893670-41-4

Library of Congress Control Number: 2009934124

A Tebot Bach book

Tebot Bach, Welsh for little teapot, is A Nonprofit Public Benefit Corporation which sponsors workshops, forums, lectures, and publications. Tebot Bach books are distributed by Small Press Distribution, Armadillo and Ingram.

The Tebot Bach Mission: Advancing Literacy, Strengthening Community, and transforming life experiences with the power of poetry through readings, workshops, and publicatons.

This book is made possible by a grant from The San Diego Foundation Steven R. and Lera B. Smith Fund at the recommendation of Lera Smith.

www.tebotbach.org

To my family for their unfailing love and support—
My mother,
Dad and Donna,
my brother, Richard
and
my dearest cousin, Bonnie Roche-Bronfman

ACKNOWLEDGMENTS

Grateful acknowledgment to the editors of the following publications in which these poems first appeared, sometimes in different versions:

88: A Journal of Contemporary American Poetry : Letter from Babylon
Ploughshares: Instructions for Life
Pool: Half-Life: Postcard to Atom, Letter to the Dark Mirror, Bulletin, Arts and Crafts: A Warning
Prairie Schooner: Before Perspective: Letter from the Body, Full Can, Feels Empty, Inklings, Letter from a Painting
Poet's Corner: Fieralingua (Italy): Letter to Mystery
Rivendell: Dispatch to Luke from Buttonwillow, Calif.
The Journal: Letter to a Stranger, Letter Under Siege
The Los Angeles Literary Review: Jacobson's Organ: A Memo

Video from the Archives was anthologized in *Chance of a Ghost*, Helicon 9, 2005

Unending gratitude to the beautiful Elena Karina Byrne for her love, her genius and her great generosity which made this book possible.

For her eternal wisdom, friendship and devotion, the marvelous Madelaine Brody.

Thanks to Brett Taylor for so much laughter. And to Sharyn and Bruce Charnas for their constant support and caring. A deep thank you to Molly Bendall, Leslie Campbell, Judith Serin, and especially Donna Prinzmetal for their invaluable assistance on the manuscript and life in general. Thank you, over and over to Tracy DeBrincat, Don DeLillo, Mialyn Hana, Robert Johnson and Judith Taylor for their inspiration and encouragement. My love to my daughter and son-in-law, Shana and Phil Buckman. And much gratitude to those who gave me light in mind and body, dear, brilliant, Eric Powell, Dr. Paul St. Amand, Dr. William Stubbeman and especially,the amazing, compassionate Dr. Dvorah Simon.

A special bouquet to my wonderful publisher, Mifanwy Kaiser and Tebot Bach!

In beloved memory of my mentor, the great poet, Stan Rice; my loving stepfather, Dr. Donald Hoytt, and my lifelong friend, Sandra Golvin.

I set up the camera at the top of the stairs and did the shot of the Beast carrying Beauty, who is tattooed by the shadows of the leaves in the moonlight.
　　　　—Jean Cocteau, *Beauty and the Beast: Diary of a Film*

TABLE OF CONTENTS

I

Written out on his body [his tattoos] were a complete theory of the heavens and the earth, in his own proper person Queequeg was a wondrous work in one volume…mysteries he himself could not read…therefore destined in the end to molder away with the living parchment upon whereon they were inscribed.
—*Herman Melville*

HALF-LIFE: POSTCARD TO ATOM

Did you know that light instructs, illuminates, but
can't see itself? That light *itself* is blind?
You always knew I'd have to be a woman
who tries to break the code of heaven's enigmatic billboard,
to reconstruct each day out of
the stolen grammar of candles.

While I sit in my white sheets as the burning
calyx of a burning lily. When I eat
certain pharmaceuticals my body spells itself
like a telegram from the Buddha,
and sometimes I hear applause.
Sometimes I can still see the oxygen/hyacinth/speechless/
Cadillac radiance of everlasting earth.

"Each atom goes through all possible histories."
I found that on the ground on the back
of a blue index card in a child's handwriting defining "half-life":
the time it takes for the disintegration of half
the atoms in a radioactive substance.
I'll tell you what I've inherited: years that go in both directions.
There is no salt divinity here, no rain.

All night I dream of a new body.
Not next to me, but my own.

LETTER TO A STRANGER
—for Don DeLillo

Now you know better,
everything's worse than before and better,
even though you're no longer brave enough
to eat raw oysters, or swim to the pier at night,
or drive the 110 with your neck half snapped off,
the ache of time pulling itself loose from the commitment
of space, the bloody frescoes and keening cathedrals
of the last fuck, the last war,

that sterile walk on the moon
while we danced the hullabaloo,
then sprinted from elevators with briefcases chained
to our wrists—breathe, dammit, breathe—
your body, a drunken specimen of repetition,
though no wine has passed your lips, says when you can't sleep—

a prayer that your mania for harm
will be snuffed out, though you feel naked in the sun inside
your house and your open-eyed insomniac asks for you—
do you read Fenallosa to find out
why the Chinese ideogram drove Pound so wild, why
he couldn't lie flat enough? Do you listen
to Thomas Bernhard's inspired whining or read
Darwin on his finches, finding the voice of a stranger
more intimate, though misdialed, than you expected?

No, you watch the Marx Brothers on roller skates
in *The Big Store*, bring anarchy into your bedroom
where it belongs, where you can stroke it, make it bigger,
which is why you no longer have a signature,
well, it's just a straight line, a way of turning
the other cheek to capitalism for you must offer
your crummy landlord something: the pomegranate
cracked open with its cache of rubies is not enough.
Have you noticed how neatly water mends itself?

You've abandoned your orchard and the ground runs
with the soft guts of crushed oranges and nearly plums.

Maybe you are your own rescuer
and you're calling to yourself
before you die of exposure, "Over here,"
just over this bridge's sudden amnesia,
"I'm over here."

VIRTUALLY YOURS

My other mouth has nothing left to say.
It's a novice again, confusing fricassee with furioso.
My other hide has no surface you would smooth
like a sheet of paper or the cool underneath
of a doll's dress.

My other eyes have no gloxinia to scarlet.
No sissy trinkets to throw into the yard.
My other hands have no rivulet
in which to mud themselves. No new
confessions to carve with apprentice ink.

My other legs no longer twine or tango
towards or away.
My other head has no honeycombed brain
to untease the skein of scheduled madness
or disappear your image like a cloud
that dissolves with my least intent.

INSTRUCTIONS FOR LIFE

Take a word, crosshair it into place
and begin its trajectory toward *l'ancien*.
Greek, Latin, hieroglyphics.

Whatness is concerned with content.
So many private horrors stink of kerosene, bloodsport.
Whereness is concerned with linkages.
We begin almost demented by the Big Bang accuracy
of metaphor. And the Word was…
Yes, we trusted the usher.

But the map—the points and symbols,
longing and attitude—
fails to deliver. It
caroms blindly into a mountain, like the young,
blonde movie star in her plane.

We are the ones who put life into stones and pebbles.
We had to invent art to understand nature.
She had to invent a self,
not to be crushed to death by it.

LETTER TO MYSTERY: THE LAW OF SIMILARS

"…because the printing is skin-deep and unalterable."
—*Walden and Civil Disobedience*, Henry David Thoreau (on tattoos)

She asked her father, "What happens
when a cobra bites a cobra?" She knew

her scarf wanted to slough off and die, heat
and sacrament flake, rise,

as she walked in gardens where
replicas of the great sculptures still

Think and Kiss, twist in their guise
of order and happiness, happy in their unlikeness

to real flesh. "They're kind of immune to each other,
so the poison doesn't hurt them," the father said, flicking

a matchbook with most of its teeth
missing. Today there must be people

who get what they want.
This much slave to that much master: Drink it up. Marry

the rush betrayal brings,
then try to love it, the locusts hungry for more years.

My lovely fix, consider this:
you can't die of shame,
but you can die of something equally invisible.

LETTER TO THE DARK MIRROR

"I'm getting to know you
one orifice at a time,"
you said, after we'd talked long
distance about sex
and vegetarianism.

I knew our relationship would always
be virtual.
No magical bewitching
of twisted syllables and sheets woven
into replicas of our muscles.
No poppy-slaughter orgasm.

But it didn't matter. I was going for
the Audrey Hepburn gestalt. Gaunt, gamine
but never naked, stripped of Givenchy
with her wrists tied to a bedpost.
You thought you could ransom my desire
over the telephone?
My hearing's too good for that.

These days I sit for hours, watch the swan
drag his dark mirror behind him.
Learn to eat what I'm handed.
Last summer, before I met you, I rode in the ambulance
and felt the centrifugal force of my life
wanting to re-enter my body.

Sorrow, after all, being commonplace.
I didn't know I'd have to let the arrows go.

LETTER UNDER SIEGE

I never stopped because I had to keep going,
        restoring words
to their paragons, not taking meanings on,
        not exactly taking them off,
like a coincidence of clothing or my flesh
        that burns of uranium,
that liquid mercury ripple effect of the gowns
        Harlow or Myrna Loy wore
in the old silver nitrate black and whites
        where they didn't even have bodies,
just velocity.

But I had to find an inventive sputtering of language
        that I could still
shout from the roof if necessary, if help came
        in that way god said it
would come during a flood, perhaps in a helicopter,
        only the man didn't take it,
but now I think I would, having figured out
        the calligraphy I call
Spain or Montana, my place on the map that I can reach,
        not merely read.

I wanted to see it coming but didn't. Not the condition,
        not the body pain, not his leaving me
for a woman sprawled on the hood of a car,
        the sinister squall of her
lipstick's dead cactus color

and the balcony lift-off of seeds
        that had been planted hard there,
with roots barely
        breathing into the earth—

hard like tonight is hard and last night was hard
        and still there's an undertow
of the literalist that takes me at times,
        this part and that part,

this arm and that hip, this ankle and that hand.
        Tonight I see it: the quantum
meeting the quantifying, the storm, the lipstick, the dolls
        whose eyes are glued open
night and day. I thought it was my job to enter
        the minutes, to let out
these images as if underwater, yet

you don't see it coming because
        time, that new spanking room,
opens right up and you go in
        whether you want to or not,
because it works that way
        and you find yourself
in a field, not of grass or light or grasslight
        or the Aurora Borealis
but of all that you'll never know
        but that could be
and is, yours.

II

Another day snatched from pain, from that huge black room from which we emerge like chimney sweeps.
　　—Jean Cocteau, *Beauty and the Beast: Diary of a Film*

LETTER FROM BABYLON

All this time I've been leading the life of the healthy,
of loam and the limbo that mimics pleasure,
like the white spaces in Cézanne,
the "diamond zones of God"
he left on purpose because colors were all
he knew for certain.
White fields of harvest.

As time dreams itself into being
and then wakes up and remembers
it's already been done.

As once I had to have sex immediately
after lunch under the pergola
and then came the talk
about Paradise vs. Presence,

and all those minutes I was living another life, opening
and shutting drawers from which I plucked
this or that metal or sequined eye-gleam.
I was champion of folding towels
and that gaze, out into the yellow room of outdoors,
the mountains with their muscled backs
upon which I climbed, unafraid.

You know how this is: it's not just the pain itself—
eating the bloody sack and the whole
child, if you must, in order
to save the others—
it's the pain of the pain.
Grief is female.

"FULL CAN, FEELS EMPTY": A LETTER
—disclaimer on the side of canned goods

I want it all to happen so it won't happen again.

No, I'm not talking about sleeping with my professors
or other women's husbands or architects who ran away
from home or ushers whose names I didn't know.

I'm not talking about brown cocaine or black beauties
or (my favorite) red-hearted Dexedrine. I'm talking about
some flammable thing that has finally, all these years later,

ignited and spreads like a drought fire out of control.
Promiscuous light that roils and riots on the wall,
unfaithful to its source, like us.

That first fall.
The world between worlds in the no-man's land
of the movie theatre exit, where I wasn't always afraid

of the toppling night and wrapped my legs around you.
Those little flecks of trapped light. Your eyes,
which were unnaturally clear like lagoons

robbed of their fish,
on me. Little by little, I wasn't addicted,
even though your notes in immature cursive
came to me, like memos from the hereafter.
I want it all to happen
so it won't happen again.

Forgive me. For squandering myself.

LOST LETTER

Tulips: but I don't know
where they came from, just as I don't know

who made the world. I am pickling roses
for next time because they'll last longer—Double
Delights. Like a woman's shellfish-colored body

preserved after a bath: all rosy-hued and white, brindled
with pleasure, like a shrimp. No, not like a shrimp
because a shrimp is boiled to death, or sometimes eaten

alive in that Japanese restaurant on San Vicente
that I won't frequent because I don't eat
anything that moves and can't run.

In that pageant of synchronized swimming
we call our dreams, I paddle out in the rain,
the tarpaulins swollen with flood,

sky with those puffy little Georgia O'Keefe clouds,
so unsentimental it makes me want to cry and this morning
I thought it might work between us if we lived in a place

like Tuscaloosa. It sounds right: a little dust on the kitchen floor,
a few tumbleweeds looking weirdly medieval as they bounce
across the yard. I wouldn't be lost if I were in Tuscaloosa

with you. I'd be safe. Loosed to the inevitable
like jazz, I'd be married to myself at last.

VIDEO FROM THE ARCHIVES

"For we cometh to judge the light paling the door, not the darkness
it obscures."
—"The New American Ode," C.D. Wright

You wouldn't kiss me in a dream last night
    because you were married.
It hadn't mattered before. I was confused,
    like I am about the difference between
cleave and *cleave.*
    I wasn't disciplined enough to grieve
in more than two languages.

I mean, we had our arms tight around camouflage
    while the litany of laundry quoted itself over
and over in the wind. Around the perimeter
    of the yard, the composer Satie was stalking, stalking
his even paces, the madness of sameness
    where music is played in the shape of a pear.

Today, in the hours without you,
    I thought about sex
in the fancy hotel, the unopened fruit basket
    burgeoning through cellophane.

After the clean-shaven rain, I tried to leap into nothing
    but the platinum leaves, the updraft of
giddy hummingbirds, so close, they would bring nepenthe
    to my brain or throw your
final laughter's confetti before me.

The minutes still progressed steadily, roundly away
    from the time of your death, just like the symmetry
of you comparing parts of my body—
    raspberry nipples, peach breasts, plum vulva—
to the fruit in our basket, a basket woven by the blind.

BEAUTY'S RECIPE

She looked in all the places she had been:
A warehouse full of toothpicks, candelabras, tokens,
the Milky Way singing its motherly opera overhead
with built-in Cage-like silence.
Malingerer!
She thought, am I no more than a blankness?
A lost ring toss?
Coffee can mutate into cherries.
Cherries into marriage.
Her trousseau finally paroled?
Forget the sun and its recipe for happiness.
Like flinging a rock from the moon,
it has taken too long to get here.
The world cobbled together, at best,
made stranger every day.
What could rouse her?
No prince, because she is never authentically asleep.

IN THE MUSEO CAPITOLINE: EXCERPT FROM THE TRAVEL JOURNALS

      During rain
in the courtyard with the huge
marble head and foot,
fragments became whole as
we imagined the immense shape
      of what had been lost.

It was a small pleasure to lick
the sequins of water from your lips, my chosen drink.
      Tell me:
how to steep a poultice, to hotwire an engine for
this stasis, for
this *elusive-inside-body*
that keeps moving
thinking it's flux.
      Delusional.
The table set like a *tabula rasa*,
the whelped-blue, soprano icebreak, the Antarctic dream
that makes cool anarchy.

      Bless us now,
in the ochre-aching Roman light,
so I can say to myself
in daytime's tangle,
in the photograph's surmise,
haven't I seen you
      somewhere before?

DO YOU SOLEMNLY SWEAR?
In 1612 a number of Bibles were misprinted and so had to be renamed.

Be me for awhile, I beg you.
We could find our own sweet equation.
Because out of nowhere, you'll grab "The Murderer's Bible"
where Jude reads, "There are murderers" instead
of "murmurers" which most lovers do at some point
during pillowed sex and the slurry rumble
as the portal of self opens, still, still, as a private,
filigreed hallucination, all the injury running
downhill to the phone booth to make that urgent
person-to-person call but the phones are always
broken, and in the past tense, like Dostoyevsky's
shorthand for tragedy.

I'll watch you sleep, innocent as all sleepers are.
One brief transaction, tapping
the metronome heart into another's, doppelganger.
Because we were young once, children fetched from their true
lives, where skin smelled of blood-rust and suckle-sap and
skin-flint. Yes, it never ended, voodoo, the nocturnal
semiphore-desire, our skull-like knuckles rapping
on the wrong doors, to seek lovers or potions, the throttling up
of sun that made the bricks in the piazza beautiful, decoded
messages of the ancient mysteries. But now,

in this new century of false cravings, glittering immortality,
the mounting flotillas of corpses, I want to wake you and say,
as it says in "The Unrighteous Bible", (as we listen to our
birdbeat bloodpulse stopped, weak as first light,)
"Know you not that the unrighteous shall inherit the Kingdom of God?"

DISPATCH TO LUKE FROM BUTTONWILLOW, CALIF.

Right now, as I'm writing to you, I smell a smell like gardenias and Ajax and the inside of a limo after sex. No, I'm not undone, though you probably think I am, because as the day grows old there's a gash in every hour and when you smell blood, it's usually someone else's. But don't mind me or the naked brocade of my body, which has been known to be radioactive, also known to smell like a courtesan's flowers and a clean kitchen—you know, that place where you should talk to yourself more, find the current that runs under the day, all the leaves shaking with involuntary light that floats among the trees and around the house that wants to be loved like a body.

I look at you over and over, when I can see you, your small Dentyne-colored nipples as you ask me to just bite them, because we keep doing this tango with the scenery even when it's not so lush, even with the water on full blast and I don't want to understand everything, or see my own face drenched in longing. Even though it's been four years since the fire and no one's any older. That's what tragedy does to you, a leap forward into a priestly chaos which is how you are supposed to remake yourself, like right now as I'm writing to you I'm waiting for you and not waiting for you, and dust erupts from the sun and rains down, covering us and our disappearing

woe. I'd call it possession, but it happens on any quiet street. I'd call it extra-terrestrial singing, but then they'd say I'm crazy but I'm not crazy because just yesterday you asked "When you don't love me any more, will you suck my dick?" and I laughed because what you meant was, then no one will get hurt and I thought, is this American life? Is this the moment we live for? Even in the non-island kitchen, where you pressed against me on the drain board without scotch or any aperitifs, just quicksilver that still circles us like chains.

BULLETIN

There is no need for her to keep quiet.
She can rummage in her Kafka garage.
Seize everything:
Paper trees whose bark peels like pages
kept in the jagged Book of the Living.
The sun like summer's flag she carries on her shoulders
so it won't touch the ground.
The contagion of silk.
He was like a cliff
she'd get to the edge of
and think she was
going to throw herself off.
She can scatter the children away from
this dangerous blue libido at the bottom of the well.
One of them will fall in anyway.

Let her beseech the fixed gods, the listening flesh,
the twin towers of Fast and Now,
when she wakes again and again to the same bleak century.
It's almost over, that sweet
irrepressible temptation to violate
whatever's good and return home
clothed with guilt.
Bring religion back to the bedroom?
Harrumph, say the gods.
It is none of our business how you spend eternity.

BEFORE PERSPECTIVE: LETTER ON THE BODY

It began with the skin. How it wanted to be wrapped
in blue ice, while all over the city the hot tectonic
plates were silently shifting, the whole bowl unstable,

as we became tourists in our own lives,
packing the wrong clothes,
unable to read the signs.

Time disappearing inside torsos, not like
the Rilkean archaic one of Apollo whose beauty
makes you change your life, but the swollen or misshapen,

the brains with synapses meddled by pollution
and Prozac, repeating over and over
that they can't eat or that nothing will satisfy

their hunger. Like one evening when the wild card
of your body was with mine, I undid your zipper,
took you in my mouth and you called me

your beautiful darling, which perhaps most men
would under the circumstance. Does it seem like
bragging to say I was good at it

from lack of practice? No teeth or fingernails.
I didn't feel cheap, in fact, I felt expensive.
Ready to enter the back rooms of abandon.

Now that you have faded into
the background of every painting before perspective,
when in medieval iconography, children were painted

to look exactly like adults, only smaller. And the phantom
weight of infinity feels heavy, close and ornamental,
then all I want is the sanity of everyday life,

the boring dishes, machines taped together
to be of use, picking off the renegade
laundry from the line.

III

After a few hours of pain, I, too, could become a work of art and perhaps provoke envy and desire.
   —*Mutilating the Body: Identity in Blood and Ink*, Kim Hewitt

LETTER FROM A PAINTING

In this quadrant of dark,
    I'm lying alone with a painting,
the song half-sung through the clothesline,
    thud of jackfruit falling, falling all night
without end, percussive, from instant to instant,
    the voices in the yard, big bruises blooming, —
or are they flowers?
    Flowers have scarlet mouths too: betina, trumpeter,
orchid artery. Bloodblooms all. That is your
    painting, the real instrument-dark,
when you see yourself in it,
    no matter what you look like.

ARTS AND CRAFTS: A WARNING

An instant jumped out of her
as if she were giving birth to time. She realized
the past was gone—and what remained?

Only salvage, a ghost-clutch
of fresh asphalt, steamy after summer rain,
love's jump-start engine, and the coyote's compromise—the look

of a kind dog-who-is-not-a-dog, like a lover she had
who smelled like goodness, who brought loaves
and fishes, change from other countries

that spilled across her dresser,
who decorated her
with silver tracery, but who practiced

the piano on other women,
until her body flayed out and became
a table of musical triads.

She read an article that said once you
used glitter
it lodged in the floorboards, the rugs,

tracked everywhere in the house,
years later you'd still find a tiny skin-glint.
You can never get rid of it.

INKLINGS

> "...an *inkling*, the diminutive of ink, once indicated a sample or
> glimpse of a written idea, and was related to an older Anglo-Saxon
> verb *imt*, to mutter.
>
>   —*Forgotten English*, Jeffrey Kacirk

Once all my pretty truths put on ugly clothes.
I was broken exponentially, so that anyone
could see the passages of dead starlight
sieved through my body.

Once I became a rabbi of rage.
For there is something holy in anger.
The climbing temperature natural in the wilderness.
Where else can you really nail down god?

Because god keeps moving, rousted
by an errant passion of its own making,
while I wave the white handkerchief
of either surrender or goodbye.

Once I woke up, my face surprised by its own openness.
Bestirred myself and went down to the river of inklings,
thinking I might catch one. But they were lighter than sighs,
weightless as commas.

Too small to be taken so soon.

A DIALOGUE BETWEEN SURREALIST AND SOUL

Like the encounter in a garden
between a piano and a Rothko.
The bruised period toward the end of his life.
Damaged plums, dirty chords.
To manage that,
pop like a cork from this sink.
What is death but sleep
without breath?
There is no proximity like an old proximity.
She had to find the magnet
before she could end
her hunger. Who would have known
she'd have to arrive ardent but useless, so
she'd have to listen lying down or
inscribe the word chariot on a locket?
Rome vanished/buried in a night.
Absurd, she thinks
that shape must be her *shape.*

THREE MEMOS

I. MISE EN SCÈNE

Whenever I need emptiness, I climb
                into the drunk uniform, take
                my invisible crutch from the closet, watch
the constellations swing their chains
and feel myself in the middle of gravity,
                where you are
just leaving, the goldfish shine of your hair,
your new verbs thrown like stones
at the windows, where we can see
                it, time, so slow it's a snapshot of stillness,

                the endless mummy-onion unwrapping,
from nothing's outpost, the sea's phosphorous zero,
where I need emptiness
and emptiness needs me, dismantled
                bite by holy bite
so that I might start again
from the absolute mosaic,
                this long-distance dark, the house sunk
in darkness, the threshing floor, bromide-bottom,
                the beauty of it.

II. REVIEWS

When I came to the coda, I realized
it was hopelessly bulletproof.
Like the president's car windows.
Or the enchased profile of the royal couple
on a coin from a Fascist country.
In every movie, I douse myself
with its pandemonium, its full metal
contraband. The rough cage
into which I willingly thrust myself.

But I am pleased with the ordering
of the vessel. The light shards
becoming a theory. The term becoming
a sentence. Impossible ever to know
the lost caress.
Ditto the coda.

III. RUN-THROUGH: A COMPOSER'S NOTE

The melody comes to me
vexed with static.
Junk noise.
What did you expect, I hear myself say,
I'm just rehearsing. When I'm awakened
I'm a child caught in a lozenge of light.
I have a task. But I forget the point of it.
"Nothing happens until something moves."
That was Einstein. Yesterday, a man called
me a gorgeous fossil.
Though it hurt, it got my attention.
So did the purple sunset, but you can't love a cliché.

IV

To break through language in order to touch life.
—Antonin Artaud, 1947

LETTER IN THE MARGIN: NOTES FOR THE OBITS.

I *Life is a fever…*

Before
> I understood what real editing was,

> I burnt
> my tongue—

which is how cigarettes used to taste—

> on coffee,

> speed,
> fecundity,
> unconsciousness,

the brew women are drinking now. But suddenly

it's the mountain whose language

> I want to be fluent in. Like

> the time I slept with a French

anti-lover and couldn't speak a word, later

became pregnant   with vernacular,

an indecipherable message, perhaps

in Zulu patois

which has only one after-thought, thumb-knot,   the capacity
                                                        to confess

when you're on your hands and knees:

that it's another kind of forgery,

the naked cargo of communion,

the wind's hypnosis-way to Cairo,

and my orphaned
music...
in soliloquy.

II *Condolences on your string of mortalities...*

I know now

my salvation lies
in unwinding the
clockbody

corposant, but (who cares
if I unwoman myself?)

in searching for
something

to inflict

on someone. Anyone.

Because

the glister-dome has been annexed. No more stars.

Soon

Firenze will be underwater.

Same goes for Amsterdam, the Hawaiian Islands, the whole

continent of Greenland.
                              That's when
                              the dead are
                              allowed on buses
and don't have to sit in the top pews of the church.

    All of this

        after

the pentimento, the ugly,

after
the epidemic silence, suffocation,

                              something like
                              a beanbag chair
                              falling on you,

after you, the subject,

the counterfeit

      touch, caused me to overlook

the simplest hazards, to stagger into doorknobs, and collide

      into edges of tables;

misremember the directions to the night mausoleum,

which

I can only visit in
my mind anyway.

I shiver from the moon's curved shell

and its bright

gospel ornaments, since

the body grieves.

I can't explain how many times a day I climb out of my own elegy.

I wrote

to you in mirror writing

so you could read the   Eternal Erotic.
Now

I live in a place

where nobody can sleep. The only bed that seems strange is mine.

III *Mirror for Sale, Never Used*

Locked in the
Beast's castle tower
with no Rapunzel-hair for a hero to scale,

I must rush to evolve,

murmuring still

that they definitely had it wrong,

because after thirty years of therapy

I remain exactly like my father and my mother.
                    In fact,

I'm not sure I've separated

from my departed dog Kajo,

                                        imprisoned in
                                        the laundry room,

untrainable, like me,

or in a cabin

in the Fern River Valley, my old Lincoln

                    floating down the highway

in a snowstorm so I have to turn back,

nauseated from altitude

                                        until the snow melts,

and just when I've decided to write

(this is the fate you, all along, must have feared)

I see the sky's blue thigh,

my reflection in the window,

                                        looking for her future,

secular, sunwashed, or speared with hope's morphine

as all of us once wished for

and probably still do.

V

Whose skin, facsimile of time, unskeins…
—Hart Crane

JACOBSON'S ORGAN: A MEMO

> "Snakes flick their tongues to aid in the process of smelling.
> Although they have no noses, they have an olfactory organ known
> as Jacobson's organ on the roof of the mouth."
> —from *Science in Everyday Things*

Forgive me, but I rarely get the chance to speak,
if that is, indeed, what this odor of ginger and pine bark, this
staccato of ultraviolet lupine, this
grape imperative means.
My breath is useless as human breath under fire-fear.

I found Cleopatra's hair clasp one charcoal afternoon
when the psalm of the creek was nearly done.
I knew it belonged to her because I could smell
the familiar odor of Caesar's sweat,
the trace of lotus oil combed through her hair.
Beauty doesn't always remember itself.
When it does, it splinters,
and by the time it realizes what it's done, it's too late.

You can't analyze my DNA but it is made from frostbite
and Sumerian sun; from gypsy litter
and the blood of martyrs.
Night loam. Storm-delirium.
From centuries of lost languages and meteors
which fell to earth unseen.

If I flick my tongue in the breezes' cadenzas,
I can smell through to the city where all is scavenged,
friable, on and on to the end of the world,
the apocalypse, when the earth sways
and we will rise up in legions,
straight as sticks.

So when you see my skin, light as a dead leaf,
skittering on the side of the road: pick it up. Save it.
Remember how close we once were.
(And believe me, we were).
Like kissing cousins.

SELF-PORTRAIT WITH MINOTAUR

It's late in this city of sparks and psalms.
No sign of the fire-eater or the clairvoyant
who can only read her own future.
They ask me how to come back
from exile where you enter the dementia
of miniature gardens with their incontrovertible mazes,
lost without Ariadne's thread.

The view from here, as always, is misleading, as you run
toward the promise of all that remains unmoving
when you are moving. How paradise outsmarts us
with its knowledge of distance, the ship bound
for an unknown port, with the unstitched
part of sky over water, the sound of a dog in love with
an ambulance, the noose of kisses around my neck.

There are moments on the esplanade, when the hypnotic
fountains cease their lashings and quiet fasts
on itself, as if in thrall to time's embargo.
Then there is nothing left to discover, because
finally, you are inside your lit life,
crisp, unghosted with newly-minted names.
You never want to leave.

NOTHING FILLS UP IN A DAY: A MEDITATION

I can't stop
thinking: Mesopotamia, the number E, a bronze tableau
of the grassy knoll, the placenta of light that covered you—
pale smile and hair—a photograph overexposed,
the universe unfurling then folding back in on itself.
This air is displaced by fallow cocoons, the counterpoint
between decorate and decimate, the wars and the war crimes,
Yeats' cold eye,
all my darling animas squealing
Me! Me! and *You! You!*
a teeming metropolis of thought-things.
I want to climb back through the window
of grace, where each pure instant
burgeons separately, in its socket.
Help me.
My rooms are small.

THE THEORY OF INCOMPLETENESS

I came to see your kind of Manhattan. We
slow-danced naked with the ziggurat of lights
flashing on the wall. My dreams, low budget films:
boom mikes showing. Out of sync looping.
My lingerie peppered with holes made by ravenous silverfish.
But I wanted to tell you the story of my life.
The night I was locked in the museum.
Smuggled food from the paintings.
Cézanne's rotten pears. Magritte's huge apple.
Rembrandt's overcooked potatoes.
I wanted to tell you about the theory of incompleteness.
That in any mathematical system
there is always a question,
that in the language of that system,
cannot be answered.
Were you cheating on me? I on you?
Do you know what troubles me most?
I'm a kleptomaniac of love.
The riverrun of my body holds other people's passion like water.
Heloise and Abelard. Verlaine and Rimbaud. Frankie and
Annette. I can't remember what we talked about in the last
fragments but it was at the intersection
of wander and lust. I want you to know I've discovered
what's code-written on all the postcards:
the hand that slaps you is the same
one that saves you, in the panoply
of stars ratcheting in and out—before
we go to our blind, borrowed fate…

DISPATCH FROM THE DANGER ZONE

If I got the story right, you said it was the long forgotten mistress,
fingernail moon or the maternal element of fire
that is Roman or Greek or accursed
from the Dark Age, but really it is
the quicksand father eating his children,
gasp of the window opening
that is an entrance
between our forms, so,

if I got the story right, from now on, we'll have to keep moving
through the ice-axe-in-the-heart principle
whipping up desire through Art, or a pillbox
filled with bright ideas, the last siren-bird, bird-serpent,
serrated psyche as in madness, or Darwin watered down
millions of years.

This is the reason the Egg of the World
might be fried or over easy,
another hour dissolves in Helsinki and
we are only the vessel, the kerosene-machine,
the encyclopedia glistening
with all its words
like stars exploding, only the blown light
doesn't reach you for centuries, you,
marooned in another city, with a lover
who whispers, "When all you have is a hammer,
everything looks like a nail."

DUPLICATE LETTER

Once we were all at the same place.   Most often, caught.

    Under the whiteness, more whiteness, under which
        is the blackness we're all afraid of

when we can't wait for things to be over: sex, contra-
        dictions, pain. The angel was you
in another template.
        The fugitive kind.   Caught between
    witnessing and perpetration.

"I'm here for you," the psychiatrist says, writing down
        the word "hopeless" for the patient.
She writes down the word "hopeful"
      for the psychiatrist.

Rilke said that every angel is terrible. She knows
        he paced the castle in the rain, unhealed
like her.   But in another tower.

It's Einstein in a thunderclap, the light that distance travels
over time, over the dead; even when she doesn't cry
    about them,   she's barred from them.

Such poverty of the senses.
The photograph, only a senseless window into a body.
It was a ritual opportunity: dismemberment is what you do
        to remember.

She hates the house. Not the temple.
She must salt her seizures.
She must wait for things to be over.
She mustn't wait.

The dead, selfish as the living,
                              won't talk to her, even in dreams.

The torn night, the hinges creaking in the old swing.

    You heard them. They sang.

BEAUTY'S TATTOO

> "Although no connection has been made between the words tattoo
> and taboo, it seems highly likely that they are related..."
> —*Mutilating the Body: Identity in Blood and Ink*, Kim Hewitt

without my heavy dress, I wear
the evidence that self-multiplies:

the kiss between Virginia Woolf and her sister,
the way they were taught to make love
with each other,
no, it did not happen like that, but it did.

There is harm in every
healing, healing in every harm, the victim's
white gloves in the detective's hands,

back-seat sex, red leather hush puppies, Ingres' "Odalisque",
irrational numbers, translations from The Universal
Book of Secrets from which I tell
what's never been told, the underclothes
of nuns who have masturbated

to Jesus, the sixteen-year-old girl clasped
on her father's lap in his La-Z-Boy, all the medicines
I've taken extruding as rubies,
faith without a geiger-
counter, an hour when I am not afraid,

a Mt. Rushmore of my exes restored
to their former perfection, or a 3-D of me at twenty
plummeting on the downslope with the tang
of salt and singe on my tongue, an unquenchable

Peeping Tom, the soiled linens of those who live
in foreign hotels, the funnel that fed me fake
breast-milk every day, the ocean's early R.S.V.P.,
the body's elegant postscript at last, now Vermeer's

eye-blink, one of Michelangelo's slaves breaking
his bonds, a wish to hurt no one,
my parent's last kiss, the last four chords
of Chopin's "Revolutionary Étude," my wish-to-kill list,

my ways-to-die list, the scattershot sex
in between relationships, the drum's tap-to
as my soldiers march back to barracks forever,
a fiery stairway that has just been
put out, and

my testimony to all I have witnessed stamped
Irrefutable on my wrist, some of us still
laughing, half-asleep in the sun.

NOTES

Beauty's Tattoo
In 1945, while directing the film "Beauty and the Beast", Jean Cocteau was stricken with a painful skin condition. In his diary about the making of the film, his pain is interwoven with both the amazing and tortuous journey of completing it. In one sequence, after the Beast has killed and eaten a fawn, smoke issues from his skin. For eight years I underwent severe burning skin and other unbearable symptoms of fibromyalgia. When titling this collection, written over the course of the illness, it occurred to me that the beauty and pain of life are (metaphorically) etched on the skin like tattoos, like images in a film, and of course, like ink on paper. Rilke's idea of beauty as the "beginning of Terror" refers to this process of pain and fear alchemized in the conscious mind.

Letter To A Stranger
This poem references Ezra Pound's use of Ernest Fenallosa's notes on the Chinese ideogram as an early way of making images through written language. Pound's founding of the poetic style of Imagism owed a great deal to his fervent reading of Fenallosa's study.

When Pound was institutionalized for his unstable mental condition, he complained repeatedly "of not being able to lie flat enough".

Thomas Bernhard, Austrian author of *Concrete, Wittgenstein's Nephew* and many other books is one of my favorite novelists. The protagonist in his books is issuing an ingenious, hilarious, profound and consummately complex *complaint* that somehow manages to be peculiarly Bernhard *and* deeply universal.

Instructions for Life
This poem owes some of its lines to Frederick Sommer's "The Poetic Logic of Art and Aesthetics", 1972.

The poem refers to actress Carole Lombard's death in an airplane crash at the age of 33. It is a philosophical meditation on the second self that women must create to survive in a patriarchy.

Letter to Mystery: The Law of Similars
This title refers to homeopathy, whereby a minute amount of a substance introduced into the body can cure a much larger and harmful but similar or analog substance.

"Full Can, Feels Empty"
I continue to be amused and inspired by the strange, shimmering double meanings of labeling. Another example is the sign I saw above a deli slicer behind the counter at a supermarket that read, "Remove hand before using."

Beauty's Recipe
"Cage-like" silence refers to the music of composer, John Cage.

Letter in the Margins: Notes for the Obits.
The title of this poem refers to the concept of a group of people in society being "marginalized", pushed to the borders of the society by having their rights denied. Marginalization can also happen to a political issue, like global warming.

"Condolences on your string of mortalities" was spoken by a young man with Asperger's Syndrome to his speech therapist when he heard of the deaths in her family.

"Mirror for Sale, Never Used", another incidence of great labeling from a yard sale.

The word *corposant* is defined as a holy body and also as St. Elmo's Fire, the light during a storm at sea.

The Theory of Incompleteness
This title refers to the German mathematician Gödel and his Theory of Incompleteness.

CATHY COLMAN received her B.A. at San Francisco State University and her M.A. at San Francisco State University. Her book *Borrowed Dress* won the 2001 Felix Pollak Prize for Poetry and made the *The Los Angeles Times* Best-seller List the first week of its release. Her poetry has appeared in *The Colorado Review, Ploughshares, Prairie Schooner, The Journal, Mudfish, The Southern Review, The Los Angeles Review, The Spoon River Review, Barnabe Mountain Review, Quarterly West, Pool, The Squaw Review, Rivendell, Contemporary 88, The GW Review, Hair-raising, The Tebot Bach Anthology, Chance of a Ghost Anthology* (Putnam/Tarcher), *Writers on Writing* (Putnam), and elsewhere.

She has won the Browning Award for Poetry and the Ascher Montandon Award for Poetry, and has been nominated for a Pushcart Prize six times. Her collaboration with composer Robert Johnson on their vocal piece honoring the fall of the Berlin Wall was presented at the Kennedy Center. She has been a guest lecturer and reader at University of Southern California, California College of Arts and Crafts, University of California at Riverside, and a featured reader at The Los Angeles County Museum of Art Poetry Series, The Getty Museum and The Museum of Contemporary Art in Los Angeles.

A former reviewer for *The New York Times* Book Review, she has also worked as a journalist/reviewer for *Artweek* and *Angeles Magazine*. She currently resides in Los Angeles where she teaches poetry and fiction in both private classes and at UCLA.

This book is set in 11 pt Giovanni book.